2016 | Prophetic FORECAST

DOUG ADDISON

2016 Prophetic Forecast
By Doug Addison

ISBN   9780982461860
ISBN   0982461860

Printed in USA by:
InLight Connection
PO Box 7049
Santa Maria, CA 93456

Cover design by Cathy Arkle.

For ordering information contact:
InLight Connection
DougAddison.com

Table Of Contents

Happy New Year

———

The Jewish New Year, called Rosh Hashanah, fell on September 13–15, 2015. Yom Kippur, (or Day of Atonement) is September 22–23, and is considered one of the most holy Jewish holidays. Even though we are no longer under the Law of Moses, God still operates on the Jewish calendar.

Historically, Jewish people believe that God examines our lives during the time between Rosh Hashanah and Yom Kippur to see if we are ready for spiritual advancement, or promotion, to a new level of maturity. Whether you are aware of it or not, this is a time when you are able to hear God more clearly and gain direction.

Here is what is written about this time in Wikipedia. com:

Heavenly books opened

"According to Jewish tradition, God inscribes each person's fate for the coming year into a book, the Book of Life, on Rosh Hashanah, and waits until Yom Kippur to "seal" the verdict. During the Days of Awe, a Jew tries to amend his or her behavior and seek forgiveness for wrongs done against God and against other human beings. The evening and day of Yom Kippur are set aside for public and private petitions and confessions of guilt. At the end of Yom Kippur, one hopes that they have been forgiven by God."

We no longer have to atone for our own sins as that was done for us through Jesus on the Cross. But God opens the Book of Life over us all each year during the time of Rosh Hashanah and Yom Kippur.

God speaks to me on a regular basis and I have to journal every day to capture it all. Years ago my prophetic friends were all having supernatural experiences around these Jewish holidays. I felt left out because I was not having them. Then God spoke to me to go back and look at my journals. To my surprise I found that I did record a lot of revelation during those times. It might not have been the exact dates and I may not have had powerful, special encounters but indeed God was speaking to me during this time. I decided to become more intentional and set aside time to focus more on hearing God during the Jewish New Year season. When I started doing this, my ability to hear God's voice radically increased. Over the last few years I have had some encounters, and God has spoken to me with specific prophetic words for the upcoming year.

From a prophetic standpoint, in 2015 the New Year actually starts after Rosh Hashanah (September 15). However, the rest of the world is on the Gregorian calendar. I am writing this book from the standpoint of both. Since most people are used to the Gregorian calendar, I released prophetic words on my blog for the year starting in January. However, I am writing this *2016 Prophetic Forecast* based on what I am hearing God say starting after Rosh Hashanah, September 2015, through the New Year which will be October 2, 2016.

The purpose of this book

I have been releasing prophetic words on my blog for over ten years. In 2015, I had two spiritual encounters in which God spoke to me to pull all my words together into book form. Because I release so many prophetic words, they can often be forgotten. Putting them together in book form allows people to remember and pray about them.

Then the LORD replied: "Write down the revelation and make it plain on tablets so that a herald may run with it." Habakkuk 2:2

God speaks in so many ways, yet most people miss it. One thing that Jesus often taught through the parables is that in the Kingdom of God we must have eyes that see and ears that hear. He was talking about seeing and hearing spiritual things so that we may come to know His voice in deeper ways. God truly is speaking all the time, but most people are either missing or not understanding what is being said to them.

I base the prophetic words and writing I do on Ephesians 1:17–19a:

"I keep asking that the God of our Lord Jesus Christ, the glorious Father, may give you the Spirit of wisdom and revelation, so that you may know him better. I pray that the eyes of your heart may be enlightened in order that you may know the hope to which he has called you, the riches of his glorious inheritance in his holy people, and his incomparably great power for us who believe ..."

The sole purpose of hearing God and the reason I release prophetic words is so that you may know God better! The closer we get to God the clearer His voice becomes. The apostle Paul compares God's wisdom and revelation to riches. And these are the true riches that

God wants to open up to you, namely, the ability to hear His voice and respond.

I also base hearing God and the gift of prophecy on the key principle of encouragement.

"But the one who prophesies speaks to people for their strengthening, encouraging and comfort." 1 Corinthians 14:3

This is what we are aiming for. When we hear the Father's voice and begin to offer words to others, the goal is that they would be strengthened, encouraged, and comforted. We have been living in a time in which there has been an abundance of prophetic words and revelation, but not enough wisdom and understanding as to the timing of them. The result of not seeing prophecy fulfilled has brought prophetic disappointments.

"Hope deferred makes the heart sick, but a longing fulfilled is a tree of life." Proverbs 13:12

My calling from God is to help you understand how God is speaking through what is called a *"now prophetic word."* A now prophetic word is something that is not for a time far off, but one that can be applied to your life right *now* to encourage you and give you guidance.

For a number of years I have been releasing *Daily Prophetic Words* as well as weekly and monthly prophetic articles and blogs. My specialty is to understand the times and seasons when it comes to hearing God. Not all the prophetic words I release will apply to everyone. But I am getting feedback from thousands of people on how they bring confirmation or encouragement to go on during trying times.

Some of the prophetic words in this book were released in 2015 on my *Spirit Connection Webcast* and blog. I have included those that are important for this year, and I also updated them to be applicable for 2016. Even though there is a date on this, it does not mean that it is limited to this year. God operates outside of time and so you can grab hold of any of the prophetic words in this book. Respond by praying and agreeing with God for it in your own life. Please share these words with others because they will help people gain greater insight into what is happening in the world and in our lives.

My hope and prayer is that you will rise above the negative clamor out there about God judging us and that this is the end of the world. Also that you will come to know God better through the prophetic words, dreams and experiences I am sharing, as well as through your own.

Prophetic Words For 2016

This year will be a time of healing and miracles for those who have suffered unjustly. We will open the year with a purging of the things that are not of God. Beliefs we hold and actions we have taken based on those beliefs are being adjusted. God has mercy and compassion for all people. He is bringing His heart to us so that we too can operate in new levels of His love and mercy.

God spoke to me that 2016 is similar to what is spoken in Psalm 116:

"I love the LORD, for he heard my voice; he heard my cry for mercy. Because he turned his ear to me, I will call on him as long as I live." Psalm 116:1–2

We are entering into a time of answered prayers. God has heard your cry and this year will bring about the fulfillment of some promises that you may have given up on.

"The cords of death entangled me, the anguish of the grave came over me; I was overcome by distress and sorrow. Then I called on the name of the LORD: " LORD, save me!" The LORD is gracious and righteous; our God is full of compassion. The LORD protects the unwary; when I was brought low, he saved me." Psalm 116:3–6

This year will bring new levels of healing to those who have suffered with illnesses and mental torment. The brokenhearted will find healing and times of suffering and anguish will come to an end. A new level of trust is coming as God releases new joy and restoration. This is from His great mercy and thankfulness and it will overtake you this year.

"Return to your rest, my soul, for the LORD has been good to you. For you, LORD, have delivered me from death, my eyes from tears, my feet from stumbling, that I may walk before the LORD in the land of the living." Psalm 116:7–9

As you enter into God's rest, it will bring new levels of God's grace and healing; you will be able to do more with less effort. Restraints will fall away and it will be a time of remembering things that were left undone.

Completing them will bring about new freedom, joy and strength. What was once a chore will now come with ease.

"Precious in the sight of the LORD is the death of his faithful servants." Psalm 116:15

It will be important to understand God's ways as there will be some key servants taken to Heaven this year. This is not to bring fear but great celebration for their lives and what they have done. It will greatly change the landscape of Heaven and bring about a major shifting on Earth as the prayers from those who are in Heaven come into agreement with those on Earth. Also the prayers of many mothers will be answered. Those who have cried out for their children and family will see answers and positive changes begin to happen.

Times of suffering and anguish will come to an end. A new level of trust will come as God begins to heal divisions and strife. The year will end with greater unity in the spirit.

The next 24 months to radical change

This year on Yom Kippur (September 23, 2015) God showed me an outline for the next 24 months. Starting on that day and going through the next two years through September 2017, we are going to see dramatic break-throughs and turnarounds. But it will require different strategies for five different groups.

"Lift up your heads, you gates; be lifted up, you ancient doors, that the King of glory may come in." Psalm 24:7

God is moving quickly and opening up some "gates and ancient doors" which are spiritual gifts, callings and lost assignments. This will usher in God's presence in unprecedented ways.

These are the five things God showed me that He is doing in the next two years. All of them are based on the number 24, which symbolizes new leadership and authority. He highlighted 24 hours, 24 days, 24 weeks, 24 months and those who are 24 years old.

24-hour promotions

We are going to have dramatic overnight accelerations with sudden promotion, blessing or advancement. This is similar to when Joseph had a radical turnaround in his life when in one day he went from obscurity to being second in command of the entire region of Egypt (Genesis 41). Joseph had been prepared for a number of years to fulfill his dreams but his advancement came within 24 hours.

Most of the ones that are being promoted in the 24-hour time frame have already suffered losses and rejection for a number of years. They have been placed on the backside of the desert because their time had not yet come. But over the next two years we are going to see many of these sudden accelerated promotions of people who were previously unknown.

24 days to advancement

When I got this prophetic word, God spoke to me that there would be promotions that would start for many people within 24 days of Yom Kippur. Yom Kippur ends on September 23, 2015. I realize this date has passed, but go back and check to see if anything significant happened or shifted into place for you on or after October 17, 2015.

24 weeks to radical change

Many people are going to see a major change in their lives 24 weeks after Yom Kippur, which is March 9, 2016. Interestingly, God spoke to me earlier that when we (in the U.S.) set the clocks forward in the spring, things will begin to spring forward in the spiritual realm. This date is March 13, 2016. This is also the timeframe of my birthday and God always does something new on that day. Watch for the first two weeks of March to bring about some radical changes.

I saw two groups within this 24-week time period. The first group was those who have been preparing and God has already taken them through a time of radical pruning and purging within their lives. This group will gain an extraordinary amount of revelation over the next 24 weeks that will position them to advance suddenly in March 2016.

The second group is those who have been on the frontlines of ministry and have taken a beating. God is calling this group to take a break, rest and regroup over the next 24 weeks. Many who do not do this will be at danger of being taken out totally. As they take time to rest and heal, God is going to re-fire them into an upgraded level that they have never seen before. This does not mean you have to take the entire 24 weeks off. God has already spoken to these leaders that they will need to take times of rest in order to move into the next phase of their lives and ministries.

24 months of amazement

The entire timetable that I was shown was from September 23, 2015 going for 24 months, which ends September 23, 2017. During this two-year period we are going to see things move at an accelerated pace. Many people who have thought they had missed God's greater calling on their lives will be strategically re-aligned for accelerated advancement. What would have taken many people a lifetime to achieve will be accomplished in less than two years. Also those who did not take time to pull back and rest will go through a time of suffering.

24 year olds

God showed me that He is moving on people who are 24 years old in 2015 and 2016. They were born in 1991–1992. Many of these young people feel like there is something greater for them to do but they are not sure yet what it is. Over the next 24 months through September 2017, God will be speaking to this group and over the next two years they will have encounters with the Lord and sudden advancement.

It is time to soar

"But those who hope in the LORD *will renew their strength. They will soar on wings like eagles; they will run and not grow weary, they will walk and not be faint."* Isaiah 40:31

This is a time of renewal for those who have grown weary waiting for things to be fulfilled in their lives.

New strength is coming that will result in advancement, promotions and sudden acceleration. Prepare to "March forth after March fourth."

We are coming out of a seven-year dry time and wilderness season in which there has been an abundance of spiritual dry bones. 2016 is the turning point in which God is reviving those who have been waiting and have not given up.

Some people have died (spiritually) in this wilderness time. There will be an opportunity to get back into the new flow of what God is doing. But because it will look dramatically different than most people are used to, it might be too much for them to understand. For those who are hungry for more, God will cause you to soar like an eagle and renew your strength.

Healing of prophetic hopelessness

Because we are coming out of a dry season in which we have not seen a lot of prophecies fulfilled, many people have fallen into prophetic hopelessness.

"Unrelenting disappointment leaves you heartsick, but a sudden good break can turn life around." Proverbs 13:12 MSG

This will change this year as God is fulfilling His promises over us. We will see sudden good breaks and longings fulfilled. During this time, God will show you which prophetic words have become outdated. There are prophecies that have been spoken over our lives that will be fulfilled. There are others that were dependent on seasons and people responding. God is renewing your hope and will speak clearly to you this year.

"If people can't see what God is doing, they stumble all over themselves; But when they attend to what he reveals, they are most blessed." Proverbs 29:18 MSG

Expect to gain new vision this year and watch for God to speak to you more clearly about your life and destiny.

Shaking happening right now

We are going to see a lot of uncertain times. This is a time of shifting and sifting in order to usher in one of the greatest moves of God in history. Many people are misinterpreting this as judgment. This shaking is designed by God to get us back on track with our callings. We must be known for our love and not what we feel disagrees with our beliefs.

"At that moment the curtain of the temple was torn in two from top to bottom. The earth shook, the rocks split and the tombs broke open. The bodies of many holy people who had died were raised to life. They came out of the tombs after Jesus' resurrection and went into the holy city and appeared to many people." Matthew 27:51–53

The shaking that is happening is going to shake open some ancient things, similar to when Jesus was crucified. The earthquake opened the tombs and brought the old prophets back to life. There has been revelation, gifts and callings sealed away for this very time. The shaking happening now is not judgment but it is going to open up the tombs that have held callings, gifts and anointings from the past.

The veil that is holding people from entering into the "Holy of Holies", or the deeper things of God, is being removed. This year we will start seeing deeper revelation and an invitation for deeper intimacy. People who were thought to not be fit to encounter God are going to have radical experiences!

Watchman being restored
Many intercessors have grown tired, and some were negatively influenced and began to judge others regarding the things they were seeing from God. This judgment caused them to lose their authority in prayer. When

God reveals something to the intercessors, it is meant for prayer, not to bring judgment.

"I have posted watchmen on your walls, Jerusalem; they will never be silent day or night. You who call on the LORD, give yourselves no rest, and give him no rest till he establishes Jerusalem and makes her the praise of the earth." Isaiah 62:6–7

God is restoring prophetic intercessors and He is also raising up new watchmen on the walls. God showed me that it is the prophetic intercessors that have prevented many terrorist attacks, although they are not aware of this. Just as terrorists often operate in "sleeper cells" in which they are not aware of the actions of the other small cells of terrorists, so it is with small prophetic intercession groups. Their efforts may go unnoticed and they often are not aware of the actions of other intercessors.

God is restoring the authority of the intercessors as they step away from using what they are praying to judge others. There is new power coming to reveal and stop the attacks of the enemy.

Reconciliation instead of accusation

The spirit of judgment and accusation has been dominating the Church for the past few years, creating an unhealthy environment. When we accuse others without trying to find solutions, we must not come into agreement with darkness over a person but instead see God's purposes for them.

One of the names given to Satan is the accuser of believers (Revelation 12:10). We need to be very careful to not accuse others but build them up instead. God is releasing a spirit of reconciliation to offset the strong negative accusation. There are many Bible verses that talk about blessing people instead of cursing them (Romans 12:14, Ephesians 4:32).

"All this is from God, who reconciled us to himself through Christ and gave us the ministry of reconciliation." 2 Corinthians 5:18

God's new agenda
God has an agenda this year to bring healing and reconciliation to people who have been wounded or rejected by Christians. There is such a large number of people who have been wounded by Christianity. God's love is for everyone and we must show it to those who need it the most. Quite often these are the ones who might be offended by us or have different viewpoints. God is drawing in the spiritual outcasts right now and dragging

a net along the bottom that will pull up people from all walks of life.

In order to be part of God's agenda we must love unconditionally and be willing to walk with people who have been rejected and wounded. Love and lots of grace is required to be part of this new move coming to the spiritual outcasts. Yes, God is on the move among the tattooed and pierced, those who are into zombies and vampires, gays and lesbians, New Age people, and those of various political parties that are currently not accepted by many Christians. God is going to move powerfully among women and minorities and promote many into positions of new authority.

The Next Seven Years

———

"Forget the former things; do not dwell on the past. See, I am doing a new thing! Now it springs up; do you not perceive it? I am making a way in the wilderness and streams in the wasteland." Isaiah 43:18–19

This truly is a time in which God is doing something totally new. We are coming out of a wilderness time and this year we will see new things spring up. It will require us to forget some of our former ways of thinking and doing things. This will be the most difficult part of entering into this new season. This will be a challenge for many people as God is taking us through a purging of belief systems that are no longer effective.

Strategic new season 2015–2022

This is the start of a new seven-year cycle and season. In 2001 we saw a shift come with the tragedy of September 11 and the escalation of terrorism. Seven years later in 2008, we saw a major financial downturn in the housing market crash causing people to lose their investments and homes. Seven years later in 2015 we are entering a new seven-year cycle and we are seeing a turnaround, though many people are not seeing or believing it.

We are now in a strategic time of God repaying us for losses in our lives. We have entered into a seven-year time of mercy and blessings from 2015–2022. This does not mean that we will not see disasters or have difficult times, but God's mercy is going to triumph over judgment.

"Arise, shine, for your light has come, and the glory of the LORD rises upon you." Isaiah 60:1

It truly is a year of breakthrough for those seeking it and I will say it again: God has issued a new seven-year season of blessing from 2015–2022. For the most part, it is the result of the prophetic intercessors crying out for mercy. In place of prophetic words of judgment that have been spoken, for the next seven years God is releasing the fulfillment of prophetic words that are based in revival and blessing. This does not mean that the world will end after 2022. You will see many of your personal promises fulfilled over the next seven years as well.

Do not be alarmed

In order to cross over into the new season that is at hand you will need to get through some slightly choppy times. Embracing the "pain of change" will help right now. Things that are happening are only setbacks if you choose to view them that way. God will even use what may seem like opposition. It is actually the wind of change that is here to bring strategic repositioning that will set you up for advancement.

The places and seasons that many have been in have been limiting you. You will need to get into a place of greater ability to stretch your spiritual wings. This will allow you to catch the new creative wave coming over the next year. You will look back later and be glad that you took the risks and paid the price.

God is coming out of the box

Many people have put God in a box (so to speak). This means that they limit Him to their own understanding or experiences. Get ready to be stretched as God is doing things that are outside of our current understanding and comfort zone. We are being challenged right now to move into new levels of understanding. A new wave of revelation is being released that will help us progress into more effectiveness.

It will require you to let go of some current doctrines and beliefs that are no longer relevant for today.

"Enlarge the place of your tent, stretch your tent curtains wide, do not hold back; lengthen your cords, strengthen your stakes." Isaiah 54:2

This stretching will enlarge things in your life more than you ever dreamed possible! Many people will be tempted to reject these new things and think they are not from God. It will require "eyes to see" and using wisdom.

We hold the keys

There are negative prophetic rumblings and many Christians are saying that the economy and the stock market are going to crash. Some people are saying that God is judging the world to its core and that He will use this crash to transfer the wealth of the wicked into the hands of the righteous.

This kind of thinking is driven by spiritual pride and it instills fear in people. We have to be careful that we do not buy into this and actually cause the economy to crash from self-fulfilling prophecies.

Yes there are difficult times and turmoil happening. People are misinterpreting what they are hearing and seeing. This is not the destruction or judgment level of a total crash. I heard God clearly and have been releasing words that we are in a seven-year season to prepare for the harvest. God is bringing a window of opportunity to finance Kingdom projects needed to bring a revival and awakening.

The Church is being shaken awake right now. God is trying to shake us to see that we hold the keys to life. We are the ones who have the keys to blessing, we can change the spiritual atmosphere, but we have to come into agreement with it. Instead people are agreeing with the plan of the enemy to destroy us before our appointed time. This is the very reason that revivals have been delayed and why we have gone into a seven-year wilderness time.

God is driving out negativity, fear and unbelief. This is a time to love, trust and step up in faith. The key to this next revival is rooted in loving people and developing Kingdom finances. I remember the late prophet Bob Jones would talk about the one billion-soul harvest. Every time he talked about it he would say, "It is going to cost a lot of money because this group is young." This is the very reason it is not the season to pull back financially. We need to get God's strategies for Kingdom financial blessings so that we can impact the world like never before.

This is part of the reason that we are getting a lot of warfare and many people have been sick and discouraged. I am not backing down on this message of love. I need your help to get it out there and change the spiritual atmosphere over us.

Hidden ones are coming forward

God has hidden many people over the last seven years. When God does this in your life, it seems that no matter what you do, things do not seem to work for you. But this is the time for you to come forward with new favor.

Watch as the hidden ones begin to emerge. These are the ones who have felt a strong calling of God and have had prophetic words spoken over them. But things have looked opposite for a number of years. Many people who have these high callings from God have been in solitary confinement and have felt that they missed it or that God does not care about them.

Going through a season that is opposite of your potential calling is quite common and it even happened to many people in the Bible. David got anointed by the prophet Samuel to be the next King of Israel. But the king at that time was Saul, who pursued him relentlessly for a number of years. Things looked opposite but then everything turned around for David and he went from being hidden to stepping into his life calling.

False humility being healed

There is a difference between when God hides you and when you hide yourself. Hiding yourself is *false humility*. When God hides you, you are still operating in all that you are called to, but God allows you to have minimal favor and people tend not to listen to you.

These hidden seasons are necessary because they help us to grow and mature spiritually. The temptation during the quiet seasons is to pull back even further and give up. But God does not want us to do this. That is false humility and so many people begin to hide themselves thinking they are being humble when in reality God wants you to move forward.

You will see healing happen for those who hid themselves or gave up. This is a time of promotion and advancement. The end result of what you are being called to might look a bit different than you first expected. Rest assured that God is still calling people who have these prophetic promises.

Loving Like Jesus

———

Jesus replied: "'Love the Lord your God with all your heart and with all your soul and with all your mind.' This is the first and greatest commandment. And the second is like it: 'Love your neighbor as yourself.' All the Law and the Prophets hang on these two commandments." Matthew 22:37–40

Jesus tells us that the greatest commandment is to love God, others and ourselves. We have gotten away from loving people like Jesus did. A judgmental spirit has entered the hearts of many people and it is one of the reasons we have not seen any major moves or revivals. God is healing us and restoring the simplistic love Jesus showed to people. God is calling us to love people that are different than ourselves. This means people of different political parties, lifestyles and beliefs.

Change in love

God is releasing a new wave of His love and mercy to help offset a negative, legalistic view of God that has gotten ingrained into many people's beliefs. A big sign of this is when you see people moving from grace and mercy to rules and judgment. God is love and He is calling us to have love and compassion.

When we stand too firm for what we believe we can lose touch with grace, mercy and God's heart for people in need around us. God is revealing these negative beliefs now. The best way to deal with it if you find yourself doing some of these things is to repent and be humble toward others.

"And now these three remain: faith, hope and love. But the greatest of these is love." 1 Corinthians 13:13

Standing for the truth without having love can move us into a place of losing touch with the heart of God for people in need. We are not called to battle with or hate people who have lifestyles and beliefs that are different than ours. Loving others is what will win people and change their hearts. We must be flexible and full of grace in this new season. Love will conquer all.

God is a loving father not an angry judge

One major change that is being released is how we view God. He is a loving Father and not an angry judge. God is not mad at you or punishing you for things you do. God is not punishing the U.S. or judging us right now. God the Father truly is who Jesus said He is.

"Whoever does not love does not know God, because God is love." 1 John 4:8

It is interesting that many people who deal harshly with those who are not Christians are most often the very ones that see Him as an angry judge. As we clear up our view of who God really is then we will live a life free of guilt. Then we can more easily receive God's love and mercy for ourselves and give it away to others.

Change in political Christianity

Jesus came and introduced a fresh new look into the Kingdom of God. He lived in a time when religion had lost its effectiveness and a cold and political religious spirit was in charge. This is very similar to our time right now. Jesus set an example for us to love people and not get sidetracked into political battles.

Jesus never took a political stand against people. In fact, His only political battle was for the Kingdom of God and not that of Earth. 2016 is a time when we will be getting back to the basics of love and the work of the Kingdom. Combining politics with Christianity is not on God's agenda in this new movement. Yes we can still be political and vote, but using politics to reject people is not God's heart. God is not with one particular party but will move on leaders who will listen to His voice and display justice and love.

Spirit of Elijah is going to come

This next move of God will require reconciliation between generations because many Christians have dealt harshly with others and have not shown mercy. Standing up for their beliefs and the truth has inadvertently pushed others farther away from God, and in many cases, into deeper darkness. We hold the keys to bringing reconciliation.

"And he will go on before the LORD, in the spirit and power of Elijah, to turn the hearts of the parents to their children and the disobedient to the wisdom of the righteous—to make ready a people prepared for the Lord." Luke 1:17

We cannot expect to see anyone turn to God without first humbling ourselves as parents and spiritual parents toward our children. It is time for the parents (spiritual and biological) to ask forgiveness for judging them for their beliefs and lifestyles. You do not have to agree with a person to love them. Extending love is a powerful weapon that has been overlooked.

Spiritual logjams

God showed me that many people are suffering from cloudy vision and confusion because they have a critical spirit. When we judge others we can block blessings from flowing to us. Consider these verses that have to do with giving:

"Do not judge, and you will not be judged. Do not condemn, and you will not be condemned. Forgive, and you will be for-given. Give, and it will be given to you. A good measure, pressed down, shaken together and running over, will be poured into your lap. For with the measure you use, it will be measured to you." Luke 6:37–38

People are suffering from spiritual logjams. For the most part it is from holding judgments against others.

"Why do you look at the speck of sawdust in your brother's eye and pay no attention to the plank in your own eye? How can you say to your brother, 'Let me take the speck out of your eye,' when all the time there is a plank in your own eye?" Matthew 7:3–4

Overall it is a time of major transition. Things are going to start to flow more freely. God is going to reveal a strategy that you need to flow in His will and timing for the next few years. God is gracious and is preparing you for increase! Remember to rise above your current circumstance and do not let anything stop you! Ask God if you have any areas of blindness due to a "log of judgment" in your eye. Ask for forgiveness and watch what will happen.

The Doorway To Your Advancement

"My command is this: Love each other as I have loved you."
John 15:12

This year is a time of promotions and advancements. In order to cross over to this new season it will require us to go through the doorway of pruning and purging. For those who have not been doing this already it might be a painful process. However, for those who have been seeking God's will and loving people, this will not take long.

We can not go into the new season without getting rid of the old ways of thinking and acting. Loving others does not mean loving only those who believe what we believe. Jesus made a radical statement when He called us to love our neighbor as ourselves. We must love those who believe and are different than ourselves.

The door to your promotion

The doorway to your promotion and advancement is through a time of deeper pruning. There are beliefs, doctrines and ways of operating that are no longer working or beneficial in this new season. God is pruning people right now. God spoke to me that we must walk through the doorway of John 15 with a time of pruning. It will result in us bearing much more fruit and ultimately moving from being a servant to a "friend of God."

"I am the true vine, and my Father is the gardener. He cuts off every branch in me that bears no fruit, while every branch that does bear fruit he prunes so that it will be even more fruitful. You are already clean because of the word I have spoken to you. Remain in me, as I also remain in you. No branch can bear fruit by itself; it must remain in the vine. Neither can you bear fruit unless you remain in me." John 15:1–4

What will remain after the pruning will be only the things that are of God's Kingdom for this particular time and season. It has to do primarily with beliefs and doctrines and the way we treat others and see ourselves in God's Kingdom.

"I am the vine; you are the branches. If you remain in me and I in you, you will bear much fruit; apart from me you can do nothing.

If you do not remain in me, you are like a branch that is thrown away and withers; such branches are picked up, thrown into the fire and burned." John 15:5–6

God's fire of purification is burning off judgmental and critical spirits. For those who are already going through this process, it will not be all that painful. But there are some that have gotten away from the true Vine. They have been taking a judgmental stance against others. They have been declaring the truth without showing love or humility. God is burning these things up so that we can become true followers of Jesus.

"If you remain in me and my words remain in you, ask whatever you wish, and it will be done for you." John 15:7

The result of this time of deeper cleansing will bring a closer relationship with God and you will have greater authority. Judgments against others have been one of the reasons we have not seen answers to our prayers. Once we are clean from this then we can again "ask whatever you wish, and it will be done for you."

"I have told you this so that my joy may be in you and that your joy may be complete. My command is this: Love each other as I have loved you." John 15:11–12

God's desire for us is to have joy, love and unity. He is healing those who have been operating in the opposite of these qualities. Love and joy will be the signs of those who are being promoted because love and joy are required in order to operate in this next move of God.

Becoming friends

"I no longer call you servants, because a servant does not know his master's business. Instead, I have called you friends, for everything that I learned from my Father I have made known to you."
John 15:15

To be a friend of God requires us to make sacrifices for others. There are times that we will need to put aside our strong opinions and beliefs in order to win someone over with love. We are not called to be intolerant but to have grace for others.

God is calling us to go beyond a "servant mode" in which we only do what we are told. He is calling us to be friends and family. The Kingdom of God is like a family-owned business in which we all have ownership. As we move closer to God's purposes we will gain a deeper understanding of the "Master's business." The purpose of this pruning is to bring us into a place of being sons and daughters of the King, ones that know God's heart of love and compassion for ourselves and others.

Invitation to The King's Table

I had a vision of a long table in heaven that seemed to stretch for eternity. God the Father, the King, was sitting at the head of the table. There were only a few people sitting at the table having a close relationship with the King, like family at a dinner table. There were so many empty chairs.

Then I saw people standing at attention like butlers or servants around the outside perimeter of the table. They were standing waiting for orders from the King. They were not aware that they were actually invited to the table. Instead they were waiting for God the King to give them the next orders for them to carry out.

I knew that these servants had sincere hearts and were saying I will do whatever God asks me to do. What they were not aware of is that God was asking them to come to the table for a closer relationship with Him and to have greater authority.

But it was their theology and belief systems that were holding them back. In many cases God had stopped speaking to some of these servants because He was waiting for them to mature and know His heart and not have to be told everything they needed to do.

Yes, we are all called to be servants and we must learn to listen and do what God says to us. This is an important stage of maturity, but we are being called to something higher than a servant. We are being invited to sit at the table with the King as sons and daughters. We are invited to be friends of God.

It is at this stage of maturity that God can turn to us and say, I want to bless what you want because your heart is in line with mine (Psalm 37:4). Most people could not fathom this and would think that it is their own soul speaking. In some cases it might be—but we will never know unless we try. God wants to bless the desires of your heart once your heart gets in line with His.

God is inviting you as a son or a daughter to sit at the table with Him. This is a time of close relationship and we do not have to wait until we get to Heaven; we can do this now. God is giving you an incredible invitation right now to advance to a higher level. We are being invited to be seated in the heavenly places

(Ephesians 2:6). The doorway to this invitation is love and humility.

God's command to us

"Greater love has no one than this: to lay down one's life for one's friends. You are my friends if you do what I command." John 15:13–14

Love is the key to all that we do. This is an over-looked commandment but God is calling us back to the simplicity of loving like Jesus did. This means to love people that are different than us. I realize I am repeating this a lot because it is such a stronghold over Christians and it is blinding them from greater things. This is part of the stretching that is coming because God is calling us to love all people and not just our friends.

"You did not choose me, but I chose you and appointed you so that you might go and bear fruit—fruit that will last—and so that whatever you ask in my name the Father will give you. This is my command: Love each other." John 15:16–17

You are being called and chosen to bear the fruit of the Spirit (Galatians 5:22–23) to help others. Love is what will get us through this new season at hand. If you have been operating on fumes then it is time to refuel with love and joy. If you have held strong opinions, judgments or anger against anyone then it is time to repent. Clear the airways so you can cross over into this new season. The doorway is through purging the old and being refreshed with new levels of love, joy and grace for others.

Spiritual Promotions

"Humble yourselves, therefore, under God's mighty hand, that he may lift you up in due time." 1 Peter 5:6

This is a time in which God is lifting up those who have been humble and have not given up. As I mentioned before, Jewish people believe that God examines our lives and decides a verdict about our fate and future that is revealed on Yom Kippur.

God looks at our heart

This year, starting after Rosh Hashanah and Yom Kippur (September 13–15 and September 22–23, 2015), God is promoting people as the Books in Heaven have been opened and this is a time in which God brings promotions to us. God spoke to me that many people thought they had missed theirs or messed up. The test over the past seven years was not about our sin and failures. This is important to understand about others and ourselves.

Many people have a condition of the heart that motivates their behavior and causes them to fall into repeated sin. Others have life situations that negatively influence them and cause them to sin. God looks at our heart and judges us based on our motives and life situations. He also takes into consideration the difficulty and type of calling we are pursuing and the assignments and demonic forces we have arrayed against us.

He considers what we have done with what He has given us (parable of the talents). He looks at our ability to love, be humble, and the things that we have overcome for Him. As a result, promotions and judgment are not easy pass or fail decisions.

This year, many people who thought they had failed are being promoted. The test over the past seven years was to get you to quit. If you are still going after God then you have passed a huge test. You will begin to see some major changes begin to happen in your life.

God is readjusting Kingdom assignments

Mantles are major callings from God that require years of preparation. Often people value mantles instead of recognizing God's assignments. But what we miss is that the Kingdom of God operates more along the lines of assignments. We are used to hearing about demonic assignments. That is because Satan imitates the things of God. We know that there are angels and that assignments are given to us to advance God's Kingdom on Earth (Hebrews 1:14).

In Acts 1:8 when Jesus spoke to the Apostles just before returning to Heaven, He gave them an assignment: they got the power of the Holy Spirit in Acts 2:17–18 and they became His witnesses in Jerusalem and all Judea. But they never ventured outside of their comfort zones and out to Samaria and the ends of the Earth.

It took ten years for God to raise up others to fulfill the assignment to Samaria. In Acts 8, it was a deacon named Phillip who went to Samaria. Then in Acts 13, Paul and Barnabas took the message of Jesus to the ends of the Earth. Notice that these were assignments, not mantles. As you step into an assignment and go through the testing, it then develops into spiritual authority. An office or mantle can further be established in your life and ministry. It takes years. And honestly, most people give up.

It is interesting that God has to raise up new people to help fulfill the advancement of the Kingdom.

Understanding promotions

When we stay with what God has called us to do then God can promote us into a closer relationship with Him. He grants us greater authority to do the work we are called to on Earth. People consider me to be a prophet but it has been decades in the making and it was not until 2010 when it started to take shape. Our gifts are more functions than titles.

I had several supernatural encounters in 2010 during which I was commissioned by God as a prophet. Then I went through three years of extreme rejection. I was banned from speaking in the churches I helped start, people lied against me, and there was jealousy and misunderstandings. I had both Christians and the occult praying against me. I ended up very sick, depressed and in debt.

But in 2013 I was given prophetic strategies to get out of debt and then the favor of God and man started to return. Jesus also visited me on August 31, 2013 and gave me new strategies for breakthrough. You do not need a visitation from an angel or Jesus to advance. I had not gotten one for decades. This usually comes later in your spiritual life when you need it the most and you are able to handle it.

Many people resist or give up during their testing times. If this happens you will adjust back down to the level of authority you can handle in your life. This is God's grace and love and not a demotion. He does not want you to die—because higher callings can indeed kill you, spiritually and physically if you are not prepared.

God is promoting you to the next level of your current sphere of influence. This does not mean that you suddenly become a prophet or apostle. It comes with steady advancement in what you are already doing. Although God is accelerating the promotions of many people, it still comes with times of testing.

Spiritual promotions coming

Oftentimes we do not recognize when we are promoted spiritually. This is because it usually is not announced, but suddenly we feel extra pressure. Think about taking on more responsibility or getting promoted in your job. You are really encouraged and feel good at first. Then you realize that the new job is stretching you, causing you to learn and use more effort.

It is the same when you get a spiritual promotion. You move into a new season where you are being stretched.

And just like with a job, there might be people who treat you differently or are jealous. This happens with the demonic realm and you may encounter some "spiritual bullying." Also the jealousy of others can dramatically impact you. Promotions are the major shifts in our life that happen after you grow from the challenging experiences and you settle into the new authority you have in the spirit.

"Those who sow with tears will reap with songs of joy." Psalm 126:5

This is a year that many people will get promoted in the spirit. There is a time of change for those who have "sown in tears." Your turnaround is here as God has heard your cries and is answering your prayers. Your sowing and *weeping* is now turning into sowing and *reaping*. Expect to see answered prayers but it might look different than you expected. Be open to your solution coming in different forms.

Gifts are being redistributed
We all have assignments and we are being sent by God to fulfill them.

"Nevertheless, each person should live as a believer in whatever situation the Lord has assigned to them, just as God has called them." 1 Corinthians 7:17

I have been seeing assignments redistributed to new people. This is because others either said no, got under warfare and quit, or other reasons. This is the time to ask God for an assignment that has been discarded and the grace to carry it out.

This year God is taking gifts and callings that people have not been using or those of people who have fallen or died and He is redistributing them to those who will use them to advance the Kingdom. This does not mean that you will get someone's mantle, but instead various gifts and assignments are being given out. It is happening swiftly.

Earlier this year I had an encounter in which an angel handed me a tarnished key that had belonged to a leader. He told me that it was the Key to Life and Death. It is similar to the Key of David mentioned in Revelation 3:7:

"... What he opens no one can shut, and what he shuts no one can open."

I used it for myself to get out of the prison of sickness I was in for several years and I am now healed. I have noticed that I have new prophetic authority when I minister. I often get "prophetic keys" of life that are used to help people. This is an example of what God is saying about the gifts being redistributed. Watch for something new to be given to you.

Welcome to the School of the Holy Spirit

Many people are being trained by the Holy Spirit right now at an accelerated pace. God is raising people up to do amazing things on Earth. Sometimes it is difficult to recognize that it is these times of testing that are actually a big part of being promoted.

Think about the lives of Joseph or David. Both of them had amazing callings from God that were announced prophetically. Then they went through years of testing and trying times during which things actually looked opposite. It was these times of pressure that brought them to a place of refinement. Many people who are going through these times are going to begin to emerge.

The most beneficial thing for you right now is to realize that everything that happens to you is being used by

God to help you mature and grow. Once you realize this, you can gain a higher perspective on your life and the trials you are facing. God did not bring on the pain or sickness. That comes from the enemy. But He will redeem it in your life if you recognize the process.

Life is never without trying times and pain. The key to it all is how you view it. If you believe everything that is happening to you is punishment from God, then the enemy has succeeded in short-circuiting your spiritual growth. If you think bad things happen to you because you must have done something wrong, then you will most likely not get out of the loop of discouragement.

The fastest way to grow and mature is to realize that God loves you and is not your enemy. Begin to see your pain or disappointments as a time of learning. You can change anything in your life right now by changing the way you view it and how it affects you. Here is some good news for you: people who have a higher calling and great destiny receive lots of discouragement and setbacks. This is because what you will learn through it goes into a firm foundation that God can build your tall calling on.

2016: Start Of The Next Move Of God

"For I will pour water on the thirsty land, and streams on the dry ground; I will pour out my Spirit on your offspring, and my blessing on your descendants. They will spring up like grass in a meadow, like poplar trees by flowing streams. Some will say, 'I belong to the LORD*'; others will call themselves by the name of Jacob; still others will write on their hand, 'The* LORD*'s,' and will take the name Israel."* Isaiah 44:3–5

God spoke to me that there is going to be a start of a major movement in 2016. I want to give you the history of this prophetic word and help you understand the season we are in right now. I have been releasing prophetic words about this for a number of years but I have not understood the timing of it until now.

11:11 a time of transition

Many people like myself have been seeing the numbers 11:11 on the clock and in other places. A number of years ago God spoke to me about the prophetic meaning to this phenomenon. Symbolically, the number eleven represents transition and revelation. We are in a time of major transition.

Throughout history, God has sent revival and major movements that seem to ebb and flow like the tides of the sea. Just as we can predict the tidal patterns, I believe that if we study the history of revivals we will find patterns and great lessons that will prepare us for future moves.

History of God moving in North America

I began studying revival patterns in North America and I noticed that we would have a major move of God's power every 11 years or so. Interestingly, you can follow this 11-year pattern from the 1906 Azusa Street Revival up to the Toronto Blessing in 1994. It actually goes back to 1884 with Maria Woodworth-Etter to 1917 with the launch of Aimee Semple-McPherson to name a few.

Here are just a few of the 11-year patterns. In 1950, there was an incredible Healing Movement in which God anointed great healing evangelists like William Branham, A.A. Allen, Oral Roberts, and many others. They would actually empty out hospitals and bring the sick to tent meetings where thousands of people were miraculously healed. Within a few years, the intensity of this healing movement subsided.

Eleven years later around 1961, the Charismatic Renewal movement kicked into high gear. Previously only Pentecostals sought the fullness of the Baptism of the Holy Spirit. During this move of God, Baptists, Methodists, Catholics, Presbyterians, and many other denominational Christians began getting filled with the Holy Spirit.

Again, 11 years after that, in 1972, God answered the prayers of many people and sent the last known major revival in America: The Jesus People movement. Hippies began to give their lives to Jesus and they poured into churches everywhere. Unfortunately, many Christians did not recognize this movement as being from God and rejected it. The hippies forever changed the way we experience church services by introducing culturally relevant music and casual attire allowing people to come just as they are and experience God's love.

Then, another 11 years passed and, in 1983, John Wimber and Peter Wagner came together and began teaching a course at Fuller Seminary on Signs and

Wonders of God for today (Course MC510). They introduced the idea that the gifts of the Holy Spirit and the power of God were not just for a few anointed leaders, but for every Christian who sought them. This was known as the Third Wave Charismatic Movement and brought the understanding that everyone is a minister whether you are in ministry or not.

Eleven years later in 1994, God brought a very unusual move called the Toronto Blessing. The Holy Spirit began to touch people with laughter and power. Millions of people from all over the planet visited the Toronto Airport Church and their lives have been renewed. We needed to laugh to break free from the religious spirit that was ruling the church at that time. Add 11 years to 1994 and it falls on 2005.

What happened in 2005?

For a number of years I was announcing to people that there would be a move of God in 2005 based on this prophetic pattern. But 2005 came and went and nothing occurred. Instead, things seemed to be the opposite. It was as if we went into a time of withdrawal. I was perplexed by this and prophet Bob Jones told me that I did not miss my prophetic words, but the understanding was hidden. Then in September 2009 I had an encounter that explained why.

The last move of God was the wilderness!

On September 8, 2009, I had a night vision in which I was taken to an aerial view of various parts of the world. I was shown vast landscapes of lush grasslands that were teeming with new life. I could see exotic plants and trees and I knew that what I was seeing was a new move from God that had come upon the Earth to bring about a radical revival.

Suddenly, a massive wave of destruction came upon the greenery. The whole scene was consumed and only a barren wasteland was left in its place. I watched in shock and felt disappointed and distressed at what I had witnessed. Then the audible voice of God spoke to me in the vision and said, "I released something new from Heaven, but my people were not ready for it, so I had to bring a wilderness time to purge things that were not of Me."

As I woke from the experience a very strong presence of God was in my bedroom. The Holy Spirit spoke to me that God planned the start of something new in 2005 that would bring about a new level of anointing.

This new level was intended to awaken a new revival. But because we were not ready for it, He changed it into a wilderness time instead.

Since 2005 many people struggled through a major time of purging, testing, and realignment. Wilderness experiences from God are necessary in order to refine and prepare us. God released many promises to people in 2005. Some promises have been delayed and are now being released.

"Therefore I am now going to allure her; I will lead her into the wilderness and speak tenderly to her. There I will give her back her vineyards, and will make the Valley of Achor a door of hope. "
Hosea 2:14–15a

Check for yourself—think back and look at the year 2005 and see if anything unusual happened. Were you going one direction when things switched and seemed to dry up? As I have asked people this question, I am hearing story after story of how God had either made a promise that did not seem to work out, or some even saw a new move of God start that suddenly got cut off.

What was your 2005 story?

Our ministry was located in Los Angeles at that time. We were gathering the resources and people to start a training and outreach center near Hollywood. We had been given a sizable grant to support the work when in 2005 it was as though every door closed for us. We eventually gave the grant back and moved to Moravian Falls, North Carolina.

We were literally placed in the wilderness (we lived in the woods of North Carolina) and we experienced a very difficult time for three years, including a very limited amount of influence and favor; and we went into debt. A few years later we moved back to California and have been anticipating and positioning ourselves for this next move of God.

Things are turning around

We are now in a time of realignment and restarting. Many prophetic words and promises got sidetracked or delayed, and some are now void because of the sudden switch in the spirit. If you have gone through difficult and unclear times over the past few years, this may very well be the reason why. Had God allowed the new movement to come in 2005 in the condition we were in, it may have destroyed us.

We saw several examples of that over the past few years as many leaders fell away from their callings or were entangled in sin. Most of them left ministry completely and some have been restored. Many of these big callings and assignments are sitting unattended.

2016 the next move of God

As I write this, we are approaching 2016, which is 11 years after 2005. This is our time to get ready for something big to come. I hope you can catch the prophetic significance of this like I have. Let us get ready to move forward!

This is the time to press in to God and ask Him for more clarity. You will need to watch for it. Those who are not paying attention may miss this fresh time of God's visitation. God is visiting our situations, our families, jobs, relationships, and ministries, and a trumpet blast is going out to call people to awaken!

Just as in previous moves of God, many Christians may be tempted to reject what God is doing because it appears messy. If we take history into account, when God moves, it is usually outside of our own understanding and comfort level.

Calling All Outcasts

———

Then He [Jesus] said to them, "The harvest truly is great, but the laborers are few; therefore pray the Lord of the harvest to send out laborers into His harvest." Luke 10:2 NKJV

I do not know a better way to describe the people that God is moving on right now. God spoke to me that this group is the spiritual outcasts because many of them have suffered rejection and wounding from Christians who have not understood them. There has been a lot of relational fallout with those outside of Christianity. This is sad because the people who need God the most have been rejected because of their beliefs or lifestyles.

In my experience many spiritual outcasts actually do not have anything against God. But most of them have something negative to say about God's people. This is very sad and if you are reading this book and you are one of the people who have been wounded or rejected, I would like to say, "I am sorry for all that happened to you and ask for your forgiveness."

The parable of the Great Banquet

The parable of the Great Banquet is a prophetic word for now. In Luke 14:15–24, Jesus told a parable of the Great Banquet in which a man was putting on a big feast and invited everyone to come. But they all made excuses and were too busy. So the man sent his servants out to invite the outcasts.

"At the time of the banquet he sent his servant to tell those who had been invited, 'Come, for everything is now ready.'" Luke 14:17

Because the ones who were invited got busy and did not come, the Master had to invite other people.

"Go out quickly into the streets and alleys of the town and bring in the poor, the crippled, the blind and the lame." Luke 14:21b

This is a prophetic word from God right now: "Come, for everything is ready." God has prepared an opportunity for us and we are being given an invitation to be part of something big that God has been planning. This represents the spiritual outcasts that God is drawing in now. This next move of God is similar to this parable. Many have been invited to be part of it but have gotten caught up in other things that are not in God's timing or His heart.

God's heart is for all people to come into the banquet. He is going to let the spiritually poor, crippled, blind, and lame be part of it. The spiritual homeless are being invited to the party. These are the ones who have been rejected by Christians and the Church.

God spoke to me that we need to understand this parable and not be too busy or distracted or we will miss the invitation at hand. God's agenda is to love people and bring healing. This includes the prodigal sons and daughters, pastors' kids, those who grew up going to church and many who are offended by or dislike Christianity.

These are the ones who are into strange things and unusual lifestyles that you might not agree with. Does this sound familiar? Many of these are our own children and grandchildren. God has been saving them for a new movement that they are called to be part of. He has not allowed them to come into the Kingdom too early because you cannot pour new wine into old wineskins or it will make a mess of things.

(Jesus said) *"Neither do people pour new wine into old wine-skins. If they do, the skins will burst; the wine will run out and the wineskins will be ruined. No, they pour new wine into new wine-skins, and both are preserved."* Matthew 9:17

Note that Jesus said, so that "both are preserved." God values the old ways and the new. He is not going to suddenly annihilate the old ways of doing things. However, God is making this new movement a priority right now. He will be shifting favor and finances to "new wine and wineskin" efforts.

God has been saving them for a new movement that they are called to be part of. We are about to see a move of God come to these groups. Like many movements and revivals in the past, many Christians will be tempted to judge it as not being from God. Pray that God opens our eyes to what He is doing and gives us His heart for people!

Healing of spiritual leprosy

In Jesus' day, there were plenty of spiritual outcasts. One big group was people with leprosy that were considered unclean and banned from worshiping God. Yet Jesus focused a lot of His time ministering to this group. Today we have our share of perceived "spiritual lepers." These untouchable, unlovable groups are all around us crying out for someone to get real with them like Jesus did.

I am not saying the people groups I am about to mention are bad people or spiritual lepers. I mean that many Christians view them this way. They are Democrats (or any political party other than our own), people involved in abortion, the tattooed or pierced, New Age, and gay and lesbian, to name just a few. God loves people unconditionally. We must heal the gap between the Church and the spiritual outcasts.

God is releasing a new anointing of power and love for those who have been unloved and unwanted by the Church. God's new agenda is to heal those who have been wounded by Christianity. Their cries for justice have reached the ears of the Lord and this is why the next move of God will be focused on the spiritual outcasts.

Sheep of a different sheep pen

"I have other sheep that are not of this sheep pen. I must bring them also. They too will listen to my voice, and there shall be one flock and one shepherd." John 10:16

God is calling the "other sheep that are not of this sheep pen." And yes, they too will awaken to the voice of

God, but it will need to come through our words spoken to them. Even though this verse spoken by Jesus was about the Gentiles, it is a prophetic word for today. The spiritual outcasts will no longer be left out. God is releasing a new language for us to speak that will heal their wounds and draw them to the True Shepherd mentioned in John 10.

Release of a new language

In the book of Acts, the Apostles were given a mandate from Jesus to touch the world.

"But you will receive power when the Holy Spirit comes on you; and you will be my witnesses in Jerusalem, and in all Judea and Samaria, and to the ends of the earth." Acts 1:8

In Acts 2, the Holy Spirit came on the disciples with power and the first manifestation was seen in a supernatural ability to speak the message of Jesus in various languages that could be understood by many people.

They were able to do this in Jerusalem and the surrounding territory of Judea. But ten years later they still had not ventured into Samaria and the uttermost ends of the Earth as Jesus had commanded them. Then in Acts 8 Phillip (not even an Apostle) went to Samaria and brought the power of God. It was the start of spreading God's love and the power of the Holy Spirit to the world.

In Acts 13, Paul and Barnabas ventured out to take the message of Jesus to the ends of the Earth. They had radical encounters. But it was still difficult for the current leadership in Jerusalem to understand this new movement. God gave them a new language and style that could be understood by non-Jewish people.

"Be wise in the way you act toward outsiders; make the most of every opportunity. Let your conversation be always full of grace, seasoned with salt, so that you may know how to answer everyone." Colossians 4:5–6

We are in a similar time right now. God is calling people to venture out and bring this same radical love and power to people today. But we cannot use the same style or language that we have used in the past. God is anointing language to supernaturally draw people to Himself. We will need to let go of our older styles of communicating and treating people harshly if we want to be part of this new movement. Our language will need to be "full of grace."

No longer an abomination

Even though Jesus instructed the disciples to take His message and power to all people, they got hung up on certain people groups. Spiritual pride and prejudice set in and it took a major spiritual encounter to heal this and ignite a new movement once again.

In the time of the early church, the Jewish people still considered many Gentiles (non-Jewish) to be an abomination when it came to the foods they ate and some of their practices. This caused a division and it prevented the Gentiles from experiencing the fullness of God. In Galatians 2 the apostle Paul corrects Peter on his prideful and prejudiced behavior.

In Acts 10 Peter had a supernatural encounter in a vision where God spoke to him to not call anything unclean that He had made clean. We need to be careful that we do not fall into the same trap that holds people back from experiencing God's love.

God is moving on a group of spiritual outcasts and He is making them clean through His love and grace. Yes, this is a radical message and it will look very messy, just as it did in the early church. Those that are currently called an abomination by Christians are going to be made clean by God.

Timothy Leary, Billy Graham and The Jesus People

During the 1960s and 70s a massive drug, free love and sex movement hit the United States. One of its leaders was Dr. Timothy Leary who got his students in Berkley,

California to take the drug LSD. He coined the phrase "Turn on, tune in, drop out."

Leary encouraged a generation to rebel and drop out of society. Then God responded with one of the last known revivals in the U.S., the Jesus People Movement. It was started by a young, very anointed hippie named Lonnie Frisbee. God appeared to him while he was on drugs and Lonnie got off drugs and began leading thousands of people to Jesus.

During this movement, many disillusioned hippies suddenly got filled with the Holy Spirit. God anointed them and they advanced quickly into operating in signs and miracles. Many Christians got jealous and tried to shut this new movement down. Many Christians considered the hippies an abomination in the site of God because of their uncleanliness and rebellious ways.

The Jesus People Movement was very disorganized and it was what would be considered a very messy time in the Kingdom. Evangelist Dr. Billy Graham stepped up and sanctioned this movement and helped bring people aboard. Dr. Graham found the language that helped people connect with Jesus. He took the saying of Timothy Leary and changed it to. "Turn on to Jesus, tune into the Bible, drop out of sin." Millions of people came to Jesus as a result of Graham's willingness to love the outcasts and speak their language.

Lonnie Frisbee exonerated

It has now been 49 years since the start of the drug movement called the Summer of Love. God is going to once again move on a group of spiritual outcasts like He did with the hippies in the Jesus People Movement. And similarly, it will appear to be a spiritually messy time and many will be tempted to reject it as not being from God.

Lonnie Frisbee was the catalyst and he was used greatly by God to bring millions of people to Jesus and forever change Christianity. He was literally written out of the church history books because he struggled with homosexuality and sadly died of AIDS. God used a broken, imperfect young man who was willing to say "Yes." Lonnie's story is about to be revealed to the world and his name will be honored for all that he did for the Kingdom of God.

Olly olly oxen free

I heard God say "Olly olly oxen free!" This is a saying in children's games and some sports. It indicates that it is safe to come back to the "home base" and your outs will not be counted against you. It is also an indicator that the sides of the game are being changed.

God is releasing a time when the spiritual outcast and those who have been wounded can come home to Him safely. We must allow a grace period for people who are different from ourselves to receive healing. The problem we have had is that there are certain conditions people exhibit that Christians will not tolerate without an immediate turnaround to full repentance. This is not how the Kingdom is designed to work. God is full of grace and He is calling us to extend love and kindness to people without judging them.

I realize this is a dangerous message, but God is a dangerous God. He often does things that are outside of our own understanding so that others can experience His love, power and acceptance. It might not come in a nice orderly fashion already cleaned up and in line with our beliefs. This is why God is stretching us right now to open things up to people that have been rejected before.

God is doing something new

If you study the history of revivals you will see a repeated pattern. God brings a new movement after the previous one has died down or has lost its effectiveness. Each move of God and revival was custom-tailored for its time and people group. So when something new comes, the previous movement usually has a hard time receiving it. In fact they often speak against it.

"Forget the former things; do not dwell on the past. See, I am doing a new thing!" Isaiah 43:18–19a

When God calls us to "a new thing" it requires us to forget the former way of doing things. This is not always easy because most people resist change. The current Church often rejects any new movement that God brings. We need to pray to have "eyes to see" what God is doing this year. We are going to see the start of many long-predicted and overdue revivals.

New Sound From Heaven

"And I heard a sound from heaven like the roar of rushing waters and like a loud peal of thunder. The sound I heard was like that of harpists playing their harps." Revelation 14:2

This is a time when you will need to take radical steps to get radical results. At the level the enemy has come against you, you will need to push back with the same intensity. Expect an increase in your spiritual gifts, dreams, visions, and supernatural encounters. This will open the opportunity for you to step up to a new level and see results for your efforts.

There will be a battle of discouragement, attacks against health and finances but you will need to press in and contend for your breakthrough in 2016. As I have been sharing this word from God with people everywhere I go, they give me a long list of reasons why they cannot do it. There is new power being released right now to break through, so take advantage of it and watch what happens.

Worship breaks things open

There is a new door open so come on up! It is time to rise above the things that have held you back. God is speaking through music.

"After this I looked, and there before me was a door standing open in heaven. And the voice I had first heard speaking to me like a trumpet said, 'Come up here, and I will show you what must take place after this.'" Revelation 4:1

God's voice sounded like a musical instrument and you can expect God to speak to you through music. New doors and gates are opening right now over your life. It is time to press in and rise above your current situation. Praising God in the midst of adversity breaks things open (Psalm 43).

New sound from Heaven revealed

I published this prophetic word previously but it is something that is happening more powerfully this year. God is releasing a new sound from Heaven. Many have been searching for it wondering if it involves certain types of musical instruments or style. Yes, but it is not limited to that.

I recently noticed a new style of worship music emerging. In fact, this new style has irritated those who do not understand it. Many people say they do not like the new worship music mentioning the word "I" as opposed to the songs' lyrics being about "Him." A few decades ago, John Wimber and the Vineyard Churches introduced the world to worship being about Him and not us! God's presence would show up strongly when we sang "to Him" and not only "about Him."

Just as in the time of the early Vineyard movement, things are shifting once again over worship music. Now there is a very strong presence of God coming when we declare who we are "in Him." These are called declarations or decrees and the songs often have the words "I" or "we" in them.

Do not mistake this new sound and movement as being self-centered. It is very Christ-centered and Heaven-centered as it powerfully brings God's presence on Earth as it is in Heaven. This new sound coming from Heaven right now is declaration-based. As we agree with Heaven's sound and declare who we are, watch as a powerful anointing comes enabling us to be all God created us to be!

God is activating angels to help you

Angels have been assigned to you and your family to accomplish your life purpose. Often, we are not aware of this so these angels are not activated in their assignments for you.

"In the council of the holy ones God is greatly feared; he is more awesome than all who surround him." Psalm 89:7

God spoke to me that there is a "council of holy ones" around each of us and He is making you aware of them. These are angels that are assigned to our family and generational lines. God is bringing His light of justice and the council of angels has been assigned to you to bring you closer to Him and open the doors to something new.

Angels come from the Throne of Heaven with assignments. The place of their origin is bathed in worship as God is being worshiped 24 hours a day (Revelation 4:8). God is bringing new revelation through music and angelic help to activate it in your life.

New revelation coming

New revelation is flowing for your situation right now. This revelation will bring about a course change that will align you with your destiny.

"So I opened my mouth, and he gave me the scroll to eat."
Ezekiel 3:2

Expect this sweet, new revelation to bring about changes in your course. As it comes, it will bring new connections, deeper insight, strategies, strength and encouragement. You will have a greater understanding on your next steps for 2016 as you act on what God is showing you. Listening to God and taking practical steps to activate what you are hearing is a key to your breakthrough.

Declarations For 2016

———

There is power in making declarations and decrees over your life that will align you with God's Word.

"You will also declare a thing, and it will be established for you; so light will shine on your ways." Job 22:28 NKJV

Here are some declarations that will help you bring radical changes in your life this year. You will find a new weapon of your warfare when you combine worship with a declaration style of music and prayer.

Here are some ideas on how to decree some of the things that are in this *2016 Prophetic Forecast.*

I declare and decree that this is a year in which God has heard our cries for mercy and things are turning around. *"I love the LORD, for he heard my voice; he heard my cry for mercy. Because he turned his ear to me, I will call on him as long as I live."* Psalm 116:1–2

I speak the opening of heavenly gates and ancient doors that will bring us into deeper relationship with You God. *"Lift up your heads, you gates; be lifted up, you ancient doors, that the King of glory may come in."* Psalm 24:7

We decree a time of renewing our strength and soaring in your presence God. *"... but those who hope in the LORD will renew their strength. They will soar on wings like eagles; they will run and not grow weary, they will walk and not be faint."* Isaiah 40:31

We declare that the times of spiritual hopelessness and disappointments have come to an end. This is a year of sudden good breaks. *"Unrelenting disappointment leaves you heartsick, but a sudden good break can turn life around."* Proverbs 13:12 MSG

Make us ministers of reconciliation to offset injustices and bring healing to people everywhere we go. *"All this is from God, who reconciled us to himself through Christ and gave us the ministry of reconciliation."* 2 Corinthians 5:18

We agree with the "new things" that will bring spiritual refreshment to those who have been in the wilderness. *"Forget the former things; do not dwell on the past. See, I am doing a new thing! Now it springs up; do you not perceive it? I am making a way in the wilderness and streams in the waste-land."* Isaiah 43:18–19

We declare a new day as God's light shines on and through us. *"Arise, shine, for your light has come, and the glory of the LORD rises upon you."* Isaiah 60:1

Help us to be stretched in order to receive all that you have for us. *"Enlarge the place of your tent, stretch your tent curtains wide, do not hold back; lengthen your cords, strengthen your stakes."* Isaiah 54:2

Teach us to love as you love us God. Jesus replied: *"'Love the Lord your God with all your heart and with all your soul and with all your mind.' This is the first and greatest commandment. And the second is like it: 'Love your neighbor as yourself.' All the Law and the Prophets hang on these two commandments."* Matthew 22:37–40

Give us wisdom to help those who need the love of God. *"And he will go on before the Lord, in the spirit and power of Elijah, to turn the hearts of the parents to their children and the disobedient to the wisdom of the righteous—to make ready a people prepared for the Lord."* Luke 1:17

Grant us the ability to forgive and not judge others. *"Do not judge, and you will not be judged. Do not condemn, and you will not be condemned. Forgive, and you will be forgiven. Give,* *and it will be given to you. A good measure, pressed down, shaken together and running over, will be poured into your lap. For with the measure you use, it will be measured to you."* Luke 6:37–38

We gladly receive any pruning needed in our lives in order for us to remain in you Lord. *"I am the vine; you are the branches. If you remain in me and I in you, you will bear much fruit; apart from me you can do nothing. If you do not remain in me, you are like a branch that is thrown away and withers; such branches are picked up, thrown into the fire and burned."* John 15:5–6

We decree that we will step into a place this year to have greater authority to see answers to the things we ask for in prayer. *"If you remain in me and my words remain in you, ask whatever you wish, and it will be done for you."* John 15:7

We are in agreement with God's promises to pour out His Spirit on our descendants and declare that we will see them grow fast and strong. *"For I will pour water on the thirsty land, and streams on the dry ground; I will pour out my Spirit on your offspring, and my blessing on your descendants. They will spring up like grass in a meadow, like poplar trees by flowing streams. Some will say, 'I belong to the LORD; others will call themselves by the name of Jacob; still others will write on their hand, 'The LORD's,' and will take the name Israel."* Isaiah 44:3–5

Open opportunities for us to see who needs that deeper touch. Use us to bring healing to people who have been wounded and rejected. *"Go out quickly into the streets and alleys of the town and bring in the poor, the crippled, the blind and the lame."* Luke 14:21b

We pray for the new sound from Heaven to be released on the Earth. *"And I heard a sound from heaven like the roar of rushing waters and like a loud peal of thunder. The sound I heard was like that of harpists playing their harps."* Revelation 14:2

We declare and decree that we will live our lives this year above all the negativity around us. We look for doors of opportunity and ask for eyes to see all that you are doing God. *"After this I looked, and there before me was a door standing open in heaven. And the voice I had first heard speaking to me like a trumpet said, 'Come up here, and I will show you what must take place after this.'"* Revelation 4:1

Closing words

My prayer for you is that you will find something in this *2016 Prophetic Forecast* that will help you in some way to press in to God for more. I want to encourage you to contend for more and not settle for less. I am agreeing in prayer for your breakthrough this year. This is a time like never before that we will need to be proactive to get to the next level.

Please stay in touch with me on my social media pages and let us know what happens in your life as a result of reading this.

Facebook: TheDougAddison
Twitter: DougTAddison
Instagram: DougTAddison

Blessings,

Doug Addison
Dougaddison.com

Additional Resources

Understand Your Dreams Now: Spiritual Dream Interpretation

Doug Addison's *Understand Your Dreams Now: Spiritual Dream Interpretation* is drawn from decades of classroom and real world experiences. It contains everything you need to get started, or to go to a new level of interpreting dreams. Includes a 300-symbol dream dictionary.

Personal Development God's Way

People everywhere want to know their life's purpose and destiny. This book was developed after Doug Addison spent a lifetime studying why some people's lives change radically and others do not. Packed full of practical examples, stories, and exercises designed to apply to your life.

Accelerating Into Your Life's Purpose

Discover your destiny, awaken passion, and transform your life with this ten-day interactive program. Designed to reveal your life's desires, remove obstacles, and create a written plan for what to focus on next. Change limiting beliefs, stop the past from affecting your future and develop a strategy to guide you towards your destiny. Includes ten audios and transformation journal.

Spiritual Identity Theft Exposed

The rise of identity theft in the world today parallels what is happening spiritually to people everywhere. People have been blinded to their true identity and the destiny they were created to live. Contains seven strategies from darkness and seven remedies to change your life forever.

Write a Book Quickly: Unlock your Creative Spirit

Whether you are just starting out or are an experienced writer, this precise book can help you get to a new level. Tap into your creative nature, learn secrets of writing, publishing tips, writing resources, exercises and more.

Dream Crash Course Online Training

Understanding dreams does not have to be difficult! Doug Addison is an expert dream interpreter who has interpreted over 25,000 dreams and has trained thousands of dream interpreters worldwide. He has developed a "Crash Course" on how to understand your dreams quickly. This is everything you need in one online program. Includes ten online videos, mp3, study guide, dream journal, symbols dictionary and more!

Prophetic Tattoo and Piercing Interpretation Online Training

Now you can learn the inside secrets to *Prophetic Tattoo and Piercing Interpretation* from Doug Addison. After years of development, Doug Addison is making this one-of-a-kind online training available to you, but only for a short while. Find what you need to get started in this new cutting-edge outreach strategy! Seven online videos, mp3s, study guide, tattoo reference cards and more

Prophetic Life Coaching

Doug Addison is a certified Life Coach and a gifted prophetic strategist. A session with his unique expertise can help with your personal life, business, family, health, relationships, personal development and even understanding your dreams.

Doug's coaching strategies help people in all areas of life. *Prophetic Life Coaching* can help you break through the common barriers that people experience in finding and fulfilling their destiny. In your one-to-one telephone session Doug helps direct you toward your divine life purpose by evaluating your current situation, getting deeper spiritual insight and identifying obstacles.

Activate Your Life Calling Online Community

Are you ready to bring lasting change in your life now? Do you want to discover and fulfill your higher calling? Do you want passion to get up each day knowing you are working towards your purpose?

Join us during this three-month interactive program to *Activate Your Life Calling.* This online coaching group is designed to bring the transformation in your life that you have always desired, whether that is helping you lose weight, getting a better job, launching a business or ministry, writing a book, or deepening your relationship with God … we provide all the support, practice and feedback you need to break through quickly! *Activate Your Life*

Calling will give you all the tools you need to succeed! See you there!

Please visit DougAddison.com.

Made in the USA
Charleston, SC
16 December 2015